First World War
and Army of Occupation
War Diary
France, Belgium and Germany

4 CAVALRY DIVISION
Divisional Troops
Divisional Signal Squadron
1 March 1917 - 28 February 1918

WO95/1158/5

The Naval & Military Press Ltd
www.nmarchive.com
Published in association with The National Archives

Published by

The Naval & Military Press Ltd

Unit 10 Ridgewood Industrial Park,

Uckfield, East Sussex,

TN22 5QE England

Tel: +44 (0) 1825 749494

www.naval-military-press.com

www.nmarchive.com

This diary has been reprinted in facsimile from the original. Any imperfections are inevitably reproduced and the quality may fall short of modern type and cartographic standards.

© **Crown Copyright**
Images reproduced by permission of The National Archives, London, England, 2015.

Contents

Document type	Place/Title	Date From	Date To
Heading	WO95/1158/5		
Heading	1917 4th Cavalry Division Signal Squadron 1917 Jan 1918 Feb		
Heading	War Diary of Signal Squadron 4th Cavalry Division From 1st January 1917 1911 To 31st January 1917		
War Diary	St. Valery	01/03/1917	18/03/1917
War Diary	Buigny	19/03/1917	19/03/1917
War Diary	Canaples	20/03/1919	20/03/1919
War Diary	Usna Hill	21/03/1919	31/03/1919
Diagram etc	Communications V D		
Heading	4th Signal Squadron From 1st To 30th April 1917		
Miscellaneous	Issued to Section		
War Diary	Albert	01/04/1917	06/04/1917
War Diary	Bihucourt	07/04/1917	13/04/1917
War Diary	Marieux	14/04/1917	30/04/1917
Heading	4th Signal Squadron From 1st May To 30th June 1917		
Miscellaneous	Issued to Section		
War Diary	Marieux	01/04/1917	17/04/1917
War Diary	Athies	19/04/1917	21/04/1917
War Diary	Hervilly	23/04/1917	30/06/1917
Heading	4th Cavalry Signal Squadron From 1st To 31st July 1917		
Miscellaneous	Issued to Section		
War Diary	Hervilly	01/07/1917	09/07/1917
War Diary	Athies	10/07/1917	13/07/1917
War Diary	Villers Carbonnel	14/07/1917	31/07/1917
Heading	4th Signal Squadron From 1st To 31st August 1917		
War Diary	Villers Carbonnel	01/08/1917	09/11/1917
War Diary	Athies	11/11/1917	30/11/1917
Diagram etc	Communications 4th Signal Squadron Fins Appendix B		
Diagram etc	Communications 4th Cav Div Athies Appendix A		
War Diary		01/12/1917	09/12/1917
War Diary	Field	10/12/1917	31/01/1918
War Diary	Athies	01/02/1918	06/02/1918
War Diary	Quevauvillers	07/02/1918	28/02/1918

WD 96 QM 5/85/1158/5

1917
4TH CAVALRY DIVISION

SIGNAL SQUADRON

(91) JAN-DEC ~~1917~~ 1918 FEB

SERIAL NO. 145.

Confidential

War Diary

of

SIGNAL SQUADRON, 4TH CAVALRY DIVISION.

FROM 1st JANUARY 1917 191 TO 31st JANUARY 1917 191

WAR DIARY
INTELLIGENCE SUMMARY

(Erase heading not required.)

Signal Squadron
4th Can Div

January 1917

Place	Date	Hour	Summary of Events and Information	Remarks and references to Appendices
ST. VALERY	1/1/17		Billets. Routine work. Trouble with line to Cavalry Corps owing to workers parties	appx
	2nd			appx
	3rd		Some trouble recurred on 4th Signal Co	appx
	4th		Field Squadron lines down — not one test high enough to clear farm carts with fully loaded	appx appx
	5–10th		Field Squadron lines low up higher	appx appx
	11–25th		Routine	appx
			Routine work	
			Heavy frosts	
	26th–31st		Routine work	

Total Telegrams 4401
DRLS 1142
Total 16143

Maximum 659
          449

A.W. Simpson Capt
4th Signal Sqn

Army Form C. 2118

WAR DIARY
or
INTELLIGENCE SUMMARY
(Erase heading not required.)

Signal Sqdn
4th Cavalry Division

February 1917

Place	Date	Hour	Summary of Events and Information	Remarks and references to Appendices
ST. VALERY	1st		Billets. Routine work. No change in communications	Appx
	26th		Lucknow Bde. having moved, detachment from squadron took over office at MOYENNEVILLE 12.30 p.m. 29th Lancers & 36th Horse after Sweep. KDG, Jodhpur Lancers & Lucknow Cav. Field Ambulance remained open	Appx
			Total telegrams for the month 4254
			" ORLS " " " 10586 TOTAL 14840
			" telephone calls " " 5502
			Daily average 530 messages
			maximum 631 26th Feb
			minimum 425 11th Feb

AM Larken Capt
4th Signal Sqdn

WAR DIARY or INTELLIGENCE SUMMARY

(Erase heading not required.)

MARCH 1917   4th Signal Sqdn

Army Form C. 2118

Place	Date	Hour	Summary of Events and Information	Remarks and references to Appendices
ST VALERY	1–18		Cme. as for previous month.	attd
BUGNY	19		Moved to BUGNY ST MACLOU. Lines in area superintending and wires from dumps. Communication to ATBERNIL 11.15 AM. Move working to SCO 4.17 PM. Comm. to Bdes by DR.	attd
CANAPLES	20		Marched to CANAPLES. Advanced Office opened 11 AM. Comm with EAR 11.5 AM via BERNAVILLE. Direct to EAR 12.30 PM. MHOW & SIALKOT – by DR	attd
USNA HILL	21		Marched to USNA HILL. Forward Office opened at 12 noon with 2nd Divn. Exchange taken over at 5.45 PM owing to length of main & condition of roads, they shd have trunks in getting thru. Comm. to MHOW & SIALKOT by DR & II Corps by move on phone	attd
"	22		Comm. to MHOW & SIALKOT by ordnance till 11.50 AM when telephone coms was established. One as an attached diagram A.	attd

1875 Wt. W593/826 1,000,000 4/15 J.B.C. & A. A.D.S.S./Forms/C. 2118.

WAR DIARY
or
INTELLIGENCE SUMMARY

Army Form C. 2118

MARCH 1917

Place	Date	Hour	Summary of Events and Information	Remarks and references to Appendices
USNA HILL	23-24.17		Comm. by phone to Fd. Sqn at IRLES 1-30 pm	
"	24th		Time observed. Broken at 11 pm	
"	25th		PIB moved. Field Sqn line extended to PIB.	
			Line dis. at 7-30 pm to PIB & Field Sqn	
			Cmv. restored 8 pm but lost his faults	
"	26th		PIt returned to Comm. Through phone 1.10 pm	
			PIB line again dis. 7 am. Comm. on a design B	
"	27th		Line party to PIB line found line dis. at within 1200 yards of their office	
			No line on served from their end. Line through to PIB 10.37 am	
"	28th		Communication as before	
"	29th		Line to PIB changed from AT 384 to AEH 788.	
"	30th		As before	
"	31st		Communication as before	
			Total men for month 16143 Telegram 4782
			maximum 650 ORLS total 11361
			minimum 276

A.A. Simpson Capt.

Communications VD 22/3/17

A

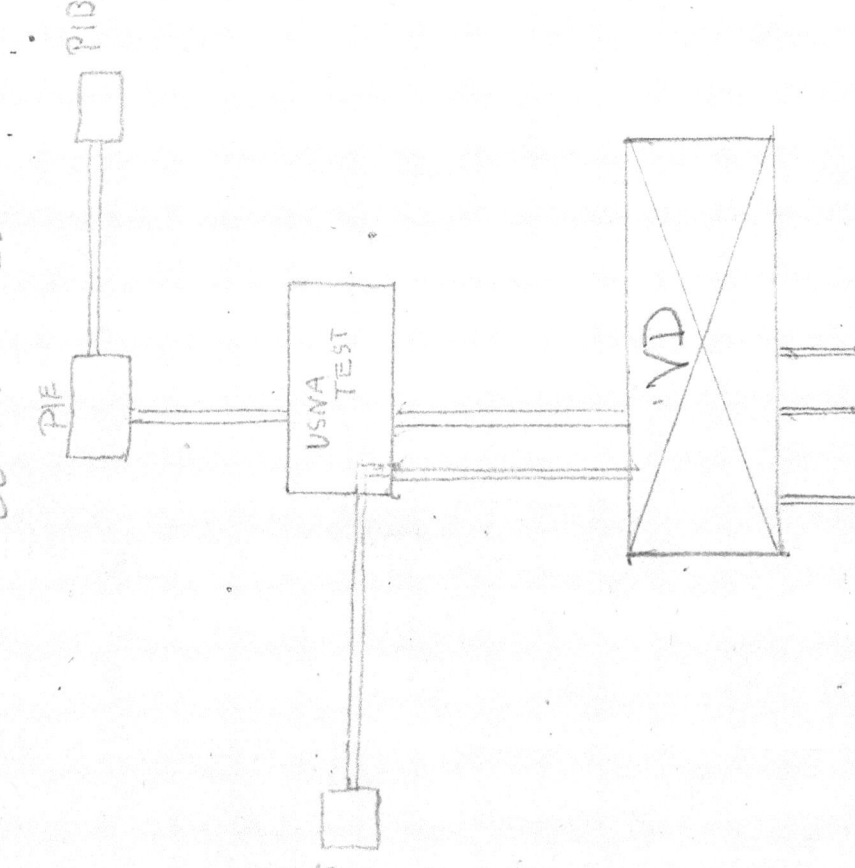

Communication V.D. "B"
26/3/17

- P.I.B.
- AT.3
- AT.4 & J.V.D.
- P/c on Bapaume Rd.
- T.U.11
- T.U.12
- P.I.E.
- Usna Test Stn.
- Y.U.1
- V.D.
- P.I.H.
- R.A.R.E.
- U.1
- Y.U.2
- "G" Staff
- "Q" Staff
- Col. Godwin's Bedroom
- Y.U.11
- E.A.R.
- Y.U.7
- Albert Exchge.

A.M.Emerson
Capt
O.C. Signals 4th Cav Div

J.M.S.

Serial No. 145.

4th Signal Squadron.

From 1st to 30th April 1917.

Daily list o

in Adjuta

Issued to Section_____

From whom.	No. and date of letter received.

Army Form C. 2118

WAR DIARY
or
INTELLIGENCE SUMMARY
(Erase heading not required.)

APRIL 1917   4th Signal Sqn.

Place	Date	Hour	Summary of Events and Information	Remarks and references to Appendices
ALBERT	1st 2nd 5th		Communication as for previous day	appx
	6th		Moved to BIHUCOURT. Comm. to 9/4th Army 10.35am. All Brigades on Telephone	appx
BIHUCOURT	7th and 8th		Communication as for 6th	appx 2
	9th		Office opened at L'HOMME MORT with communication to 5th Corps, Cav. Corps and 4th Cavt. Div.	appx
"	10th		Marched to L'HOMME MORT 2-30am. Report Centre opened there at 6-30am. Closed at 7-30am. Office at BIHUCOURT remained open	appx
"	11th		Report Centre opened at L'HOMME MORT 6-30am Closed 6-30pm Office at BIHUCOURT remained open	appx appx 2
BIHUCOURT	12th & 13th		Stationary	appx
MARIEUX	14th		Closed at BIHUCOURT 12noon opened MARIEUX same hour. 9/4th Army and AHOW Bde and IVERNON Bde Communication direct. SALROT Bde through Sigt. Army	appx
MARIEUX	15th 24th 25th		Stationary Comm. as for 14th SALROT Bde to AUTHIE direct on telephone	appx appx "
	26-30th		Stationary	appx

T. and Telegrams   4629
DR's   9430
                14059

max. 609 (7-6-17)
min. 178 (11-4-17)

A.A. Lupon   Capt.
4th Signal Sqn.

Serial No. 145.

4th Signal Squadron.

From 1st May to 30th June 1917.

Daily list of

in Adjutant

—oo

Issued to Section ____

From whom.	No. and date of letter received.

Army Form C. 2118

WAR DIARY
or
INTELLIGENCE SUMMARY

(Erase heading not required.)

4th SIGNAL SQUADRON

4th Army Sgt.

MAY 1917

Instructions regarding War Diaries and Intelligence Summaries are contained in F. S. Regs., Part II. and the Staff Manual respectively. Title Pages will be prepared in manuscript.

Place	Date	Hour	Summary of Events and Information	Remarks and references to Appendices
MARIEUX	1st–15th		Communication to all brigades – Fifth Army – Advanced Cavalry Corps. work	
March	15th		Closed MARIEUX 10.30am opened TREUX same hour. work	
			Comm. to QUERRIEUX and XIV Corps	
March	16th		Closed TREUX 11AM opened BRAY same hour. Comm. to QUERRIEUX. work	
March	17th		Closed BRAY 11AM opened ATHIES same hour	
			Comm. to Fourth Army.	
ATHIES	19th		Comm. to III Corps in place of Fourth Army work	
	20th		Comm. to Cav Corps in place of III Corps	
	21st		Comm. to all brigades by phone	
HERVILLY	23rd		Forward R.E opened at 9am	
			Communication to all brigades by phone.	
			All forward communication made metallic.	
HERVILLY	24th–31st		Total messages for month 18121	
			Telegram 5336	
			DRLS 13785	

Maximum 1130 – 25th (two offices)
Minimum 193 – 16th

A.M. Simpson Cpl.
4 Signal Sqdn.

Army Form C. 2118

WAR DIARY
or
INTELLIGENCE SUMMARY

(Erase heading not required.) 4th Signal Squadron

Place	Date	Hour	Summary of Events and Information	Remarks and references to Appendices
HERVILLY	1st		Communication as for previous month.	
	2-9th		Routine work.	
	10-20th		Several thunderstorms. Lightning protection satisfactory.	
	21-26th		Routine work.	
	27th		Move to SIALKOT Brigade stopped from 8am to 4pm, and visual and wireless satisfactory. Area WAZA	
	28-30		Routine	
			Messages for the month	
				Average
			Totals Telegrams 8348	278
			DRLS 17803	593
			26151	871
			Maximum 1104 on 3rd inst.	
			Minimum 750 on 4th inst.	

W. Anderson Capt
4th Signal Sqdn

Serial No. 145.

4th Cavalry Signal Squadron.

From 1st to 31st July 1917.

Daily list of

in Adjutant

Issued to Section

From whom.	No. and date of letter received.

WAR DIARY
or
INTELLIGENCE SUMMARY
(Erase heading not required.)

4th Sig Sqn
4th SIGNAL SQUADRON

JULY

Place	Date	Hour	Summary of Events and Information	Remarks and references to Appendices
HERVILLY	1-9		Communication as for previous month.	
ATHIES	10		Opens 9 A.M. Telegraph and Telephone to Lechon Bde at Le Mesnil, Nelson Bde at Enemain, Dieekel Bde at St. Christ H.	
			Rosina.	
"	11-13			
VILLERS CARBONNEL	14		Communication to all Bdes and Z.C.O (Cav Corps) to Cavalry Corps Closed and 3rd Corps opened at Le Cartel & Rosina.	
"	15			
"	16-31		Messages for the month	
			Telegrams 5119 Average 6.6 po	Maximum 1121 on 4th Minimum 351 on 26th
			D.R.L.S 13978	
			Total 19097	

J.B. Wolf Lt
4th Signal Squadron

Serial No: 145.

4th Signal Squadron.

From 1st to 31st August 1914.

Army Form C. 2118
(27)

WAR DIARY
or
INTELLIGENCE SUMMARY
(Erase heading not required.)

4TH SIGNAL SQDN

AUGUST

Instructions regarding War Diaries and Intelligence Summaries are contained in F. S. Regs., Part II. and the Staff Manual respectively. Title Pages will be prepared in manuscript.

Place	Date	Hour	Summary of Events and Information	Remarks and references to Appendices
VILLERS CARBONNEL	1st–3rd		Billets. Communications as for previous month. Quiet	
			Totals for month	
			Telegrams 3729 / 3	
			DRLS 11929	
			15652	
			Maximum 588 19th August	
			Minimum 397 8th August	
			[signature] Capt. 8th Cavalry	
			4 Signal Squadron	

SIGNAL SQUADRON
4TH
CAVALRY DIVISION

WAR DIARY
or
INTELLIGENCE SUMMARY

Army Form C. 2118
Army Serial No. 145

1917 - Serial
4th Signal Sqdn

SEPTEMBER

Place	Date	Hour	Summary of Events and Information	Remarks and references to Appendices
VILLERS CARBONNEL	1-30-14	1-30	Communication as for previous month	W2
			Messages for month	
			TOTAL 9945	
			DRLS 3480	
			Telephone / Telegrams 13425	

A.W. Simpson Capt
8th Cavalry
4th Signal Squadron

Army Form C. 2118
14

WAR DIARY
or
INTELLIGENCE SUMMARY
(Erase heading not required.)

Instructions regarding War Diaries and Intelligence Summaries are contained in F.S. Regs., Part II. and the Staff Manual respectively. Title Pages will be prepared in manuscript.

October 1917   4th Signal Squadron

Place	Date	Hour	Summary of Events and Information	Remarks and references to Appendices
VILLERS CARBONNEL	Oct 1-31		Communications as for previous month. Messages for month — DRLS 10280, TELEGRAMS 3747, 14027	

G. M. Biol ?
Lt. Signal Squadron
Ht Qr. 4 Cav. Division

Army Form C. 2118

WAR DIARY
or
INTELLIGENCE SUMMARY
(Erase heading not required.)

NOVEMBER 1917 4th Signal Squadron

Place	Date	Hour	Summary of Events and Information	Remarks and references to Appendices
VILLERS CARBONNEL	1–9		Routine. Communications as for previous month.	anne
MARCH	10th		Office closed VILLERS CARBONNEL opened ATHIES same hour	anne anne
ATHIES	11th–19th		Routine. Communication as on Appendix A.	anne
	20th		Report to opened FINS 12 noon Comm. as on App. B.	anne anne
	21st		R.C. opened at FINS 7 AM	anne
	23rd		R.C. closed at FINS 10 AM opened at ATHIES same hour	anne
	25th		R.C. opened at VILLERS FAUCON 8.30 AM — using 55 Div'l Office closed at VILLERS FAUCON 3.30 PM reopened at ATHIES same hour	anne anne
	30th		R.C. opened at VILLERS FAUCON 12.45 PM Cav. Corps in same place	anne
			Totals for month Telegram 4168 / 9706 / 13 874 DRLS Maximum 600 24th Minimum 256 27th	A. Wordsworth Capt 4th Signal Sqdn

Communications 4th Signal Squadron Fins. 21/11/17   Appendix B

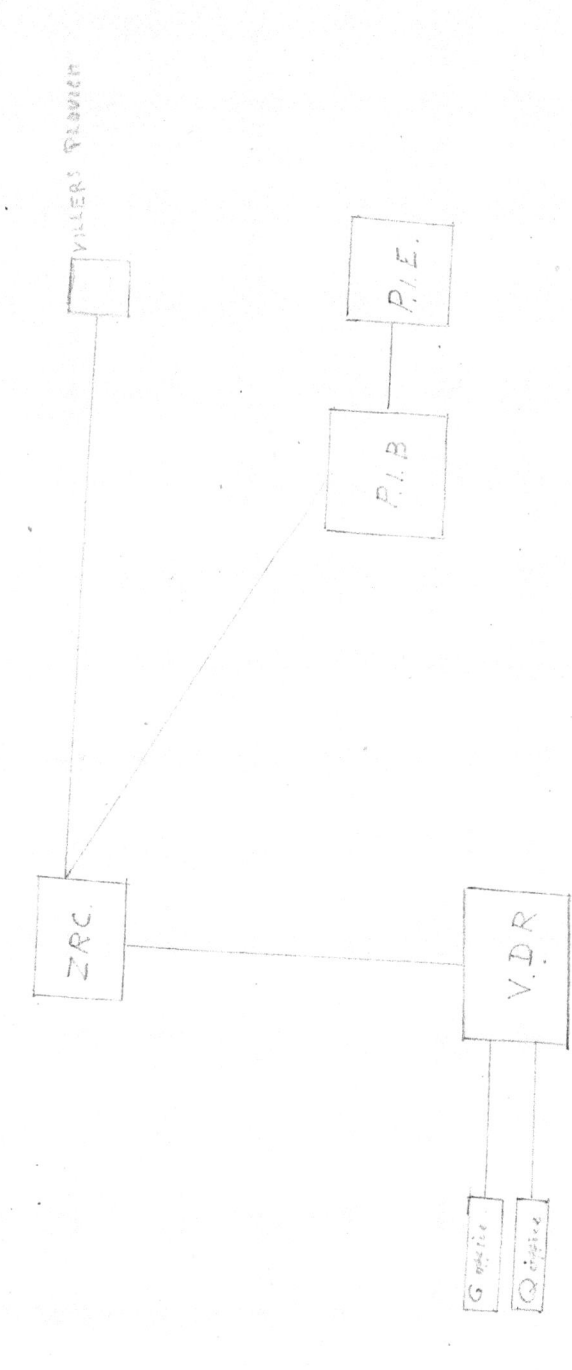

W H Simpson Capt
4th Signal Sqd.

Appendix A

Communications 4th Corps 10" Athies 19/11/17

1917 Army Form C.2118

4th Signal Sqdn.

145

DIARY or INTELLIGENCE SUMMARY

(Erase heading not required.)

DECEMBER

Date	Hour	Summary of Events and Information	Remarks and references to Appendices
1st	6-30 AM	R.C. opened Sheet 62c E5c 1.9 6-30 AM	
	6-30 AM	Telephone to Can Corps	
	3-0 PM	" " Sialkot Bde	
	2-30 PM	" Visited Lucknow Bde	
2nd		Much trouble owing to transport cutting lines	
		Communication in to Hennin elm	
	9.0 AM	Visited Mhow Brigade 9.0 AM	
3rd	9-55 AM	R.C. closed E5c 1.9 Reopened ATHIES 9-55 AM	
8th		Capt. W.E. CAMPBELL, 34th Poona Horse, took over command	
9th		Capt MTH EMPSON proceeded to take command of Cav Corps Signal School	
		On TUESDAY night RHQ signal and section left for duty under 16th RHA Bde in the line	

WAR DIARY
or
INTELLIGENCE SUMMARY

(Erase heading not required.)

Army Form C. 2118

Instructions regarding War Diaries and Intelligence Summaries are contained in F.S. Regs., Part II. and the Staff Manual respectively. Title Pages will be prepared in manuscript.

Place	Date	Hour	Summary of Events and Information	Remarks and references to Appendices
Field	10.12.17 to 20.12.17		DECEMBER Nothing to report. Training of classes carried on. "A" class consisting of 1 N.C.O. from each Regt (refresher class). Class B consisting of 1 Offr 6 or 8 of 1.E.N.g. Signalmen who had suffered heavy casualties in Signallers in the afternoon of the 1st 2nd. A practice route between two practice signal offices constructed by the classes for instruction in installation in lines was testing & fitting up of a small office.	W6
	30th		Lt. TUCZEK and R.H.A. Signal Subsection returned from the line with all stores except cable which was taken over. Regimental Grenade for R.H.A. take wires to A Signals.	
	31st		No change. Memo. Maj. Hunter. Telegram 3839 DRLS 9388 Daily average Tel: 1, 2, 3, 8 DRLS 302. 8	

W. Campfield
Captain
O.C. 4th Cavy Signal Sqn.

Army Form C. 2118

WAR DIARY
or
INTELLIGENCE SUMMARY
(Erase heading not required.)

4 DIV

Place	Date	Hour	Summary of Events and Information	Remarks and references to Appendices
Field	Jan 1st		Nothing to report. Training of signallers carried on at regt-l brigade and Div=	
	28th 29th		A dismounted Div. Signal Section formed in accordance with instructions from G. and A.D. Signals Eastcorps proceeded to HERVILLY under Capt. Atkinson O.C. no ot. Sqn 4th Cav. Div.	
	29-30th		Nothing to report.	
	31st			

	Max.	Min.	Daily average	Total
Telegrams	181	113	142.5	4270
D.R.L.S.	396	223	330	9926
Phone	321	178	241	7223

M. Campbell Capt.

SIGNAL SQUADRON.
4TH
CAVALRY DIVISION.
No. O.N. 33
Date 4-2-18

Army Form C. 2118

WAR DIARY
or
INTELLIGENCE SUMMARY
(Erase heading not required.)

FEBRUARY 1919

Instructions regarding War Diaries and Intelligence Summaries are contained in F.S. Regs, Part II. and the Staff Manual respectively. Title Pages will be prepared in manuscript.

Place	Date	Hour	Summary of Events and Information	Remarks and references to Appendices
ATHIES	1st		Communication as last month. YW	
"	2nd		When Bde closed ENNEMAIN 7.10 Ah. opened at MARCELCAVE by O/C D/R. YW	
"	3rd		" MARCELCAVE opened into L of C area. YW	
"	4th		Sialkot Bde closed ST CHRIST 8.30 Ah. opened at MARCELCAVE by O/C D/R. YW	
"	5th		" MARCELCAVE opened at CREUSE. YW	
"	6th		4 Signal Squadron closed ATHIES 11 Ah. opened GUEVAUVILLERS same hour. Telegraph and phone to Sialkot at CREUSE, to Pulham at COURCELLES, to Cavalry Corps & D/R to Lucknow at MARCELCAVE. YW Telephone to Lucknow at ST SAUFLIEU thro' Amiens civil Ex. YW	
NOYEVAUVILLERS	7th to 25th		Communications as for 7th. YW	
"	26th		Sialkot closed at CREUSE 7.20 Ah, reopened MARSEILLES same hour. No D.R.L.S. to them, sending despatches by post. Line put thro' to 19th Lancers 7.20 Ah. YW	
"	27th		19th Lancers closed 2 Ah. YW	
"	28th		Secunderabad Bde at CREUSE on telephone 2.10 Ph. YW	

Total for month: Telegrams 3,684
DRLS 9411 Telegrams 131.57
DRLS 275.39

Daily Average Telegrams Maximum 193 on 22nd
Minimum 87 " 4th
DRLS Maximum 355 " 1st
Minimum 87 " 4—

YWhite
Lt. for Capt & OC
4th Signal Sqdn.

1875 Wt. W593/826 1,000,000 4/15 J.B.C. & A. A.D.S.S./Forms/C. 2118.